ANIMALIA

Graeme Base

Within the pages of this book
You may discover, if you look
Beyond the spell of written words,
A hidden land of beasts and birds.

For many things are 'of a kind',
And those with keenest eyes will find
A thousand things, or maybe more —
It's up to you to keep the score.

A final word before we go;
There's one more thing you ought to know:
In Animalia, you see,
It's possible you might find *me*.

— Graeme

For Robyn

Canadian Cataloguing in Publication Data
Base, Graeme, 1958–
Animalia

2nd ed.
ISBN 0-7737-2756-6

1. English language – Alphabet – Juvenile
literature. I. Title

PZ7.B29An 1993   j421'.1   C93-094336-8

Published by Stoddart Publishing Co. Limited
34 Lesmill Road
Toronto, Canada M3B 2T6
First published in 1987 by Irwin Publishing Inc.
Printed in Hong Kong through Bookbuilders Ltd

An Armoured Armadillo Avoiding An Angry Alligator

Beautiful BLUE BUTTERFLIES basking by a BABBLING BROOK

DIABOLICAL DRAGONS
DAINTILY DEVOURING
DELICIOUS DELICACIES

GREAT GREEN GORILLAS
GROWING GRAPES IN A
GORGEOUS GLASS GREENHOUSE

Horrible hairy hogs hurrying home-ward on heavily-harnessed horses

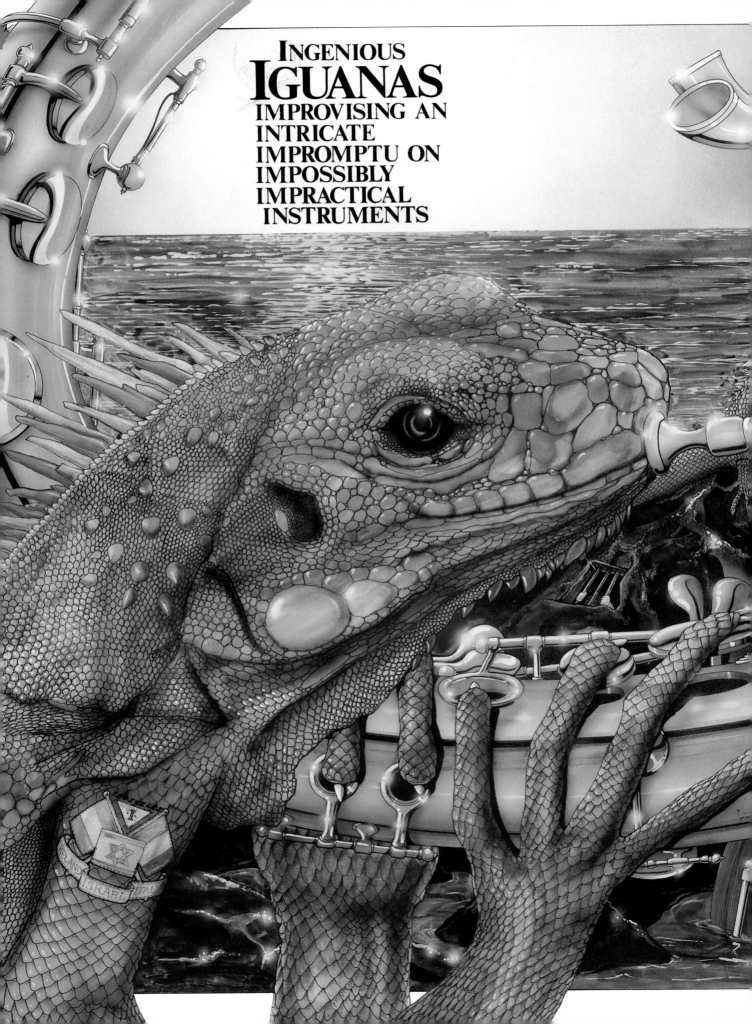

INGENIOUS IGUANAS
IMPROVISING AN INTRICATE IMPROMPTU ON IMPOSSIBLY IMPRACTICAL INSTRUMENTS

JOVIAL · JACKALS · JUGGLING · JUGS · OF · JELLY · IN · THE · JUNGLE ·

?123+=METICULOUS MICE MONITORING MYSTERIOUS MATHEMATICAL MESSAGES

Nine Nautical Newts
Navigating
Near Norway

ONE
OUTRAGEOUS
OLD
OSTRICH
ORDERING
AN
ONION
OMELETTE

Quivering Quails Queuing Quietly for Quills

RICHLY ROBED RHINOCEROSES
— RIDING IN —
RICKETY RED RICKSHAWS

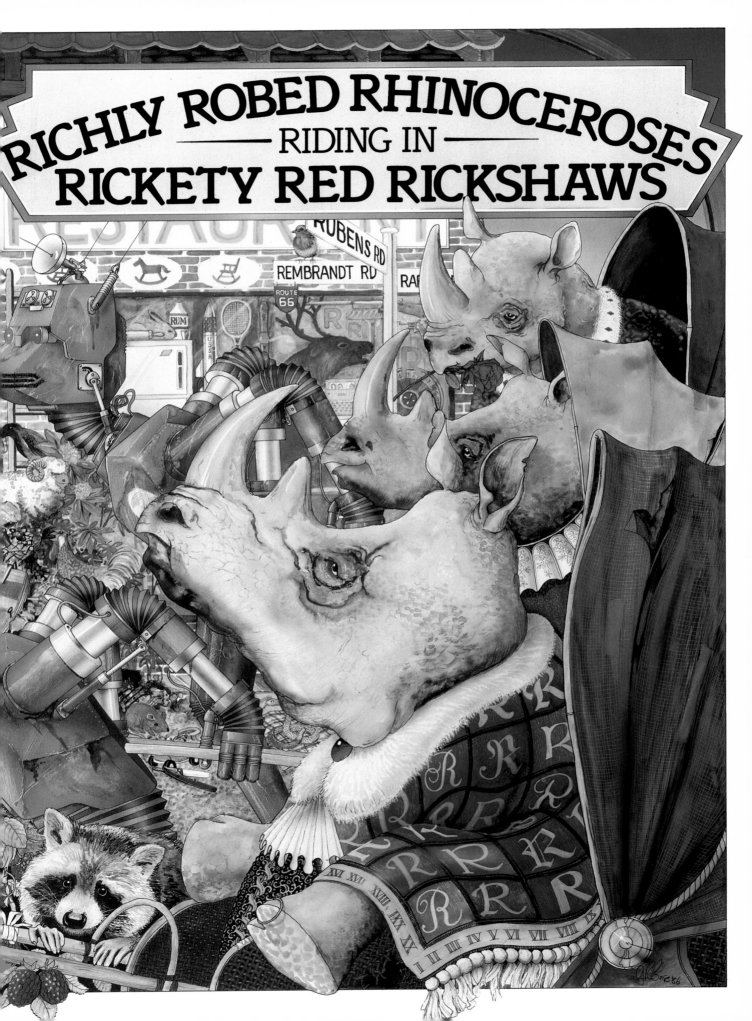

SIX · SLITHERING · SNAKES

SLIDING · SILENTLY · SOUTHWARD

SLIDING · SILENTLY · SOUTHWARD

SIX

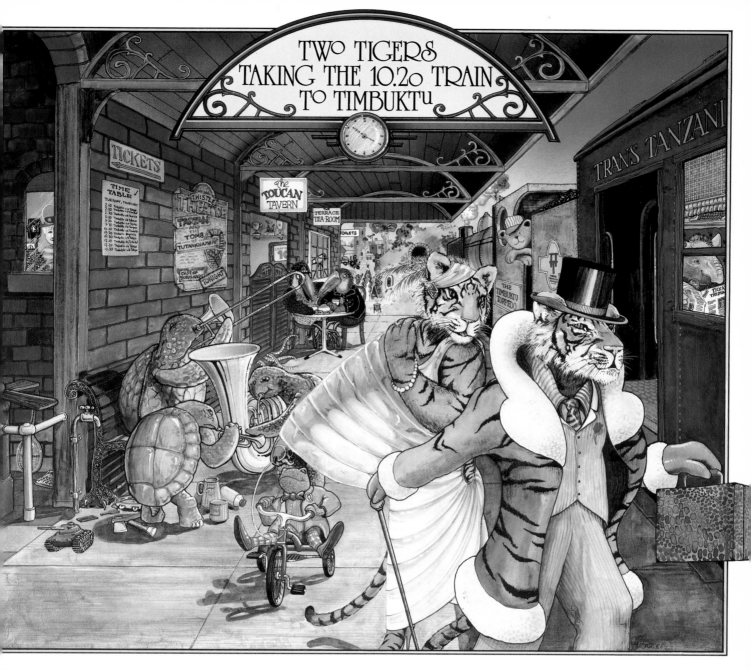

TWO TIGERS TAKING THE 10.20 TRAIN TO TIMBUKTU

UNRULY UNICORNS UPENDING URNS OF ULTRAMARINE UMBRELLAS

Wicked
Warrior
WASPS
wildly
waving
Warlike
Weapons

**YOUTHFUL YAKS YODELLING
IN YELLOW YACHTS**

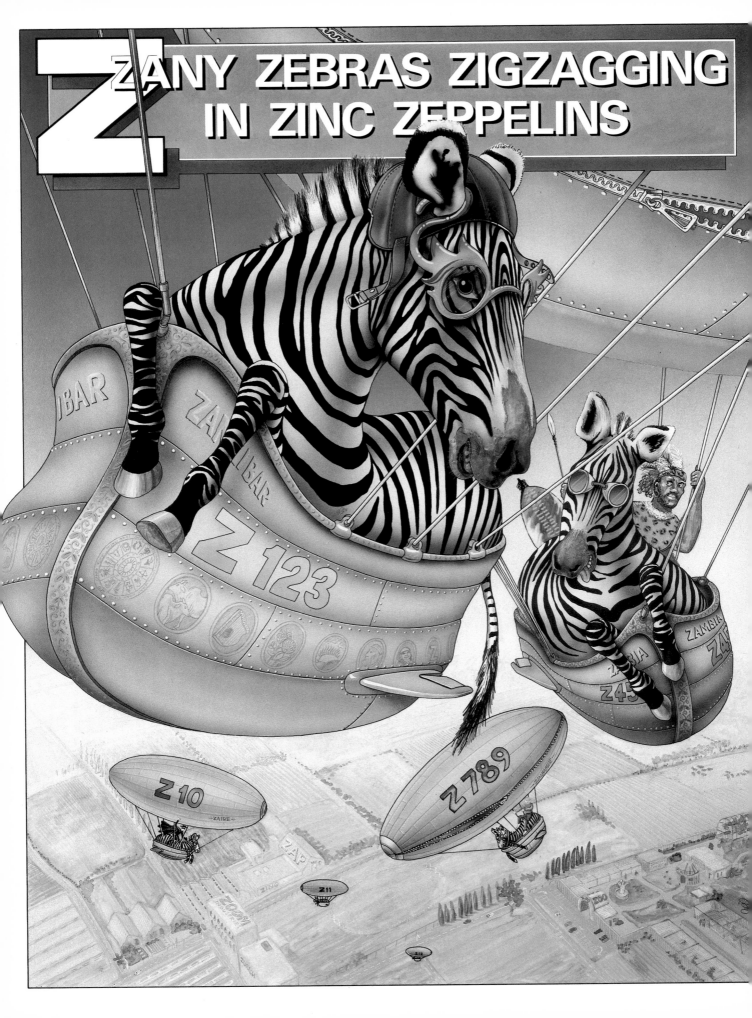

Z: ZANY ZEBRAS ZIGZAGGING IN ZINC ZEPPELINS